Thirty Day Devotional
for the
Horse Loving Girl

Jessi Ruiter

ISBN 978-1-0980-3615-7 (paperback)
ISBN 978-1-0980-3616-4 (digital)

Christian Faith Publishing, Inc.
832 Park Avenue
Meadville, PA 16335
www.christianfaithpublishing.com

Printed in the United States of America

INTRODUCTION

My name is Jessi Ruiter. I'm nineteen years old and, what can I say, I'm your typical horse crazy girl. The only things I love more than horses are my family, my friends, and my Lord Jesus Christ. Except for the occasional movie marathon, I'm a very active person. Along with riding horses, I enjoy writing, playing basketball, baseball, and well, basically anything that has to do with physical activity.

I am number three out of six kids. I have four brothers, and one big sister and being the middle child, I constantly had something to prove to them. My childhood consisted of playing in the woods, roughhousing with my brothers, getting in trouble (I was and still am quite the rebel), and working to afford my own horse. I love jeans, dirty boots, hunting, chocolate, and any color that's neon. I'm typically a quiet person, but that's not always the case. I'm scared of clowns and hate losing at anything. I'm a normal girl! I have doubts, fears, and more than my share of issues. I don't have it all together, and on my own, I never will. But by God's grace, I pray that I can take a little of what I have learned in my short life and encourage you a little bit in these thirty days.

So, grab your Bible and a pen, sit down somewhere comfy as we go, what i like to call, horse-seeing around together through some life lessons of love and fear.

DAY 1

Mucking the Stalls

Well, now that you have learned a little bit about me, let's turn on our "horse-seeing" eyes and see what we can learn about God and ourselves from our furry horse friends.

Let's start with what we know about horses. Most people who aren't around horses very much would say something like they're big fuzzy pets that they want to have in their garage. But we, horse girls, know the truth. Horses are awesome, but they are a lot of work. They cost a lot of money and make a lot of messes that we have to clean up. After all the fun riding is over, that unpleasant job of mucking out the stalls is always waiting for you.

There couldn't be a lesson for us to learn from a job as lame as cleaning out the stalls! Well, I think there is. Let's think about this for a minute. We are the masters of our horses, right? They make messes, and we clean everything up for them. It's what we do, we love our horses no matter how messy they get.

Well, if we are Christians, then God is our master, and by sending His son to die for us, He cleans out our stalls. And let's face it, we humans are professionals at making messes; I know I am at least. I make mistakes, I let people down, and I sin a lot. And I can't clean it up by myself. But God, being the amazing God He is, gave us a way. That is why John 3:16 is one of the most quoted verses from the Bible. This is the verse that lets us know that God loved us so much even with our messes. He sacrificed His only son on a cross so that our stalls will be forever clean.

Now, this is something that most of us already know, but after Jesus died, people didn't just stop sinning. The gift of a clean stall was given to us, but how do we keep it that way? No matter how hard we try, we can never keep ourselves from sinning again and again. That's why when we accept Him into our lives. He gives us His Holy Spirit to remind us of the price He paid and to keep us humbly on our knees, coming back to Him, day after day. In Mathew 16:24–25, Jesus tells His disciples to take up their cross and follow Him. He wants us to do the same, to come to Him, confess our sins, and then follow Him, daily!

Just like our horse's stall, cleaning it one day isn't enough. It must be cleaned day after day, and that can be hard. But just like cleaning up after our horses, the Lord will clean up after us if we ask Him. He's always willing, I know I don't take advantage of His help as much as I should, but once we learn to make it a daily habit, we are ready to begin exercising our faith.

Q: Do you ever find yourself taking the Lord's greatest gift for granted?

Challenge: Come up with a few ways to remind yourself daily of the price He paid to make you clean. Write a word or verse that reminds you, put a sticky note on your mirror or bed, whatever you have to do. Then thank Him for it.

> For God so loved the world that He gave His
> one and only son. That whoever believes in Him shall
> not perish but have eternal life.

—John 3:16

DAY 2

Lunging lessons

Now I meet a lot of new horses, and with every new horse I meet, I always like to work with them on the ground before I ever get in the saddle. I like to see how they move, how focused they are, and learn some of their quirks. The main piece of groundwork I use to do this is called lunging. Not everyone who has a horse lunges. For those of you who may not know, lunging is a technique to train horses to always be in tune with their master, no matter what is going on around them. The horse is asked to work at the end of a long lunge line, walk/trot/canter, circle, and respond to its master's commands in the center.

If we have our "horse-seeing" eyes on, it's quite easy to see where our lesson comes from today. Just like a horse, our lives should revolve around our master. We must respond to the commandments from our Father God as we go through our everyday lives. While we are in the comfort of our daily "routine," the Holy Spirit speaks to us. And just like our horses, we are expected to move. We need to be attentive to His voice and be ready to move from our "routine" and do what is asked of us.

If lunging is done correctly, the horse learns to settle down and focus only on its master. A horse must be completely in tune with its master, and their commands, for the ride to be successful. Just as the horse needs to focus on its master, we as children of God need to be able to solely fix our eyes on Him. God should be in the center of everything we do.

We tend to get distracted by things of this world, what others are doing, or by what we think will bring us happiness; things on the outside. But we need to look to our Master, who is on the inside, and keep Him in the center of everything we do.

Q: How attentive are you to your Master? Will you be ready to leave your "routine" when He asks?

Challenge: You have tools to help you stay in tune with your Master. The Bible is one, and prayer is another. Take time today to not only talk to your Master, but to listen.

> You will keep in perfect peace those whose minds
> are steadfast because they trust in you.
>
> —Isaiah 26:3

DAY 3

Testing the Fence

My horse paddock has an electric fence. Whenever we put a new horse in a new place, we enjoy watching them smell everything out. They run around and have to look at everything, and when they see the fence, they like to get up close. They get closer and closer until—ZAP! Then they jump away from the shock and rarely do they ever touch it again.

Horses have their boundaries. They have to see how far they can go. But no matter how far they push the limits, they will always be met by wood or wire. Whether it takes them one time or ten, they will eventually learn where the boundary is.

The same is true for us in life, only it tends to take us way longer to learn. God gave us His laws and boundaries in His word, the Bible, they are called the Ten Commandments and the golden rule, and He tells us to meditate on them day and night (Josh. 1:8). Only then does it say we can succeed and prosper.

Q: Are you like me and like to get as close to the fence as you can? Why do you think that is? And what can you do about it?

Challenge: Think of an area in your life where you push on the fence. Then pray and ask the Holy Spirit to awaken within you and help keep you away from that fence.

Trust in the Lord with all your heart and lean not on your own understanding; in all your ways submit to Him, and He will make your paths straight.

—Proverbs 3:5–6

DAY 4

Dependence

My family loves animals. Whether they are dogs, cats, or chickens, they have always been at our house. Ever since I can remember, I've always had to put in my share of the work to take care of them. One of the first things I ever learned was that I shouldn't eat until the animals have eaten, and the animals always came first. Even before I got my first horse, my dad made a deal with me. He said that the only way I could get the horse was if it would be completely my responsibility and that I would always feed it and care for it.

Having any kind of pet makes us carry more responsibility. Whether it is a horse or a goldfish, our animals at least have to eat, right? Our pets are dependent upon us to take care of them. Unfortunately for them, we are not perfect, and we don't always deliver. Sometimes, we find an angry horse or goldfish wondering where their chow is.

Now, if we put on our "horse-seeing" eyes, we can see that just like our pets, we have a caretaker. We need our caretaker badly whether we admit it or not. Lucky for us, He's a perfect Master and knows exactly what we need, whenever we need it.

The Bible tells us story after story of the Lord, delivering and caring for His followers—by saving them from a fiery death (Dan. 3) and providing them with meal after meal (Exod. 16). He cared for them, all of them. Another whole book could be written about the Lord's deliverance. If our Master can do all that, why do we still doubt? Why do we worry so much about our needs? The Lord takes care of the birds in the air, so surely He will take care of us because we are made in His image. We make mistakes, and yet our horses still wait on us to care for them because we are all they know and trust. Maybe we should learn from our pets and trust that our Master will deliver.

Q: Do you find yourself worrying about silly things, or planning your own life without thinking about the one who gave it to you?

Challenge: Our God knows the number of hairs on our heads! It's time we give the power of our lives back to the one who gave it to us in the beginning. I challenge you to write down as many of your worries as you can think of. Pray over them and then ask God to take them from you. After that, destroy the list any way you want. Rip it, bury it, and throw it away. Use any means to symbolize that they are no longer yours to worry about.

> And my God will meet all your needs according
> to the riches of His glory in Christ Jesus.

—Philippians 4:19

DAY 5

Tender Feet

Now, we all know that being a follower of God and depending on Him in all things is not all sunshine and rainbows. Just like what I said about having a horse in the first chapter, it's not all fun and games. In fact, it gets harder from here. The Lord never tells us anywhere in the Bible that everything will be better when we give our lives and worries to Him. No! He actually tells us the opposite. God said that we will be hated for our faith in Him. Right about now, you're probably thinking, *Why should we trust Him then, if things are just going to get hard?* the answer is: the same reason we work so hard with our horses. Because in the end, it's worth it. It's worth our pain and it's worth the hard work.

But just like our journey with our horses, we will hit some rough patches sooner than we think we will. I once had a horse with super sensitive feet. Every little stone he stepped on would bruise his feet, and the only thing I could do to help him was to let him take a break and give him a few days to heal.

Sometimes, we "step on some stones" in life and get bruised, and sometimes, we want to quit. Other times, we think we are strong enough to power through the pain life puts on us. But God tells us in His Word that we don't have to do either of those things. He says, "Come to me, all who are weary and I will give you rest" (Matt. 11:28). Just like my horse, when you get bruised up by all the ugly things in your life, it hurts. Stop, rest, and remember why we are here (Matt. 28:19). Also, remember that God feels all our pain and is always right by our side.

Q: Do you try to power through your pain in unhealthy ways? Or just try to forget about it? What do you do when something in your life hurts you?

Challenge: Try going barefoot on a gravel road or stony area. How far can you make it before it hurts? We can't go any further than that in our lives without taking a break and leaning on God. Next time life hurts you, remember the road; stop, rest, and cling to the one who can always get you through it—your heavenly Father.

> And teaching them to obey everything
> I have commanded you. And surely I am with
> you always, to the very end of the age.

> —Mathew 28:20

DAY 6

Bur Under the Saddle

Have you ever seen a cowboy put a bur under a horse's saddle in the old western movies? We laugh at the horse as it bolts and bucks the rider off faster than they can get on. Well, I've never put anything under a horse's saddle before, but I do know that there is a lesson in it if we look in the right place. A bur is little, and yet it bothers a horse so much, and it can't get away from it. Don't we have the same problem in our lives sometimes? Little things that shouldn't bother us crawl into our lives and under our "saddles," and no matter how much we buck or bolt to get rid of them, they hold on.

Think about the way your sibling treat you, how much stuff you have, where you were born, or how many friends you have; think for a minute about how unimportant those things really are. We were put here for one purpose, to give glory to God. If we follow Him, giving Him glory is all that should really matter. I know that is easier said than done! It's forgotten so easily, thrown into the back of our minds. All because of what? Something that didn't go the way we wanted it to!

We get so wrapped up in the things that we want to happen, and we forget that the lives we have aren't even ours to control. Those little things are just distractions, worldly burs put under our "saddles" by the devil himself. Let's stay focused girls! Let's pray, be in the word, and not let the little burs of life sneak under our "saddles" (Col. 3:2).

Q: Are you like me and get burs under your saddle easily? What distractions does Satan throw at you, and how do you deal with them?

Challenge: Write down some of your biggest distractions, and then write down things you can think about or do to get rid of those distractions.

Seek first the kingdom of God and His righteousness.
And all these things shall be added to you.

—Mathew 6:33

DAY 7

Time-Out

When my horses are naughty (which all horses are at some point) and I'm finished with my ride, they get what I call, "tie time," or what most people would know as a "time-out." Time-outs are used to make you think about where you went wrong, why you did it, and how you are going to fix it. This is a tough subject for me because the only way to make things right after you have done wrong is to admit, then submit. Growing up, I felt like I was always in some kind of time out because I didn't have the humility to admit I was wrong, and that someone else was right. It took me a long time to realize it, but there will always be someone to submit to on this earth. The sooner I learn to swallow my pride and admit it, the better off everyone will be.

We all have a place in what I call "the chain of submission." As believers in Jesus Christ, we must submit to Him first and foremost. Some of the first commandments He gave us are honor your father and mother and respect your elders (Exod. 20:12; Heb. 13:17). That gives us a huge list of more people to submit to! Thankfully, God didn't put us at the bottom of the chain. God gave us our younger brothers and sisters to look after, and let's not forget our animal friends. The only way to get them to submit is to show them that you can submit to *your* elders. So, remember that next time your little brother or sister won't listen to you. It all revolves around you and your submission to the Lord and His commandments. Admit and submit, and you will gain respect from your animals, elders, and from your God above.

Q: Are you like me and struggle to admit and submit? What do you think is holding you back from submitting?

Challenge: Write down a prayer, asking the Lord for whatever you need to be able to admit, and then submit. Then, if you feel there is someone you need to submit to, approach them and apologize for not submitting. Through prayer seek to do better.

> Because of the service by which you have proved yourselves, others will praise God for the obedience that accompanies your confession of the gospel of Christ, and for your generosity in sharing with them and with everyone else.

> —2 Corinthians 9:13

DAY 8

Natural Response

Let's talk about something that we horse girls have come to see at least once in our lives: spooking. Spooking is that horrible jump that your horse does that seems to come out of nowhere and then leaves just as quickly. It's the same feeling we get when someone jumps out from behind a corner or door to scare us.

The only thing is, horses were created a little differently than we were. Horses are called flight animals. This means that is something scares them, no matter how ridiculous it is, they believe it's going to eat them; it's their natural response. Horses see themselves as prey to everything. Whether it is a barking dog or the plastic bag flying across the yard, they still see it as a life-threatening predator. Now I know it's not quite the same kind of fear, but don't we have the same natural response to our fears sometimes? Don't we tend to be creatures of flight now and then? We fear trying out for the team and talking to someone new at school or church, and we may also experience the fear of failure or the fear of pain.

Sista that fear is of the devil! Satan has planted that inside you to keep you from reaching your full potential for the kingdom of God. The Lord tells us in His word that we were not given the spirit of fear, we were given the power of love that can defeat any of your fears. We were not created to be creatures of flight like our horses.

The only way to defeat your fear is the same way you train your horse to defeat theirs. You have to face the fear. That takes a lot of courage! But if you ask for it, God will give it to you. We all have fears, even the bravest of us. Are you courageous enough to face yours in the name of Jesus?

Q: Think of one of the things that you're most afraid of doing. Why are you afraid to try to do it?

Challenge: Pray and ask God to give you courage and faith to put that reason behind you, and then face your fear!

> Have I not commanded you? Be strong and courageous.
> Do not be afraid; do not be discouraged, for the Lord
> your God will be with you wherever you go.
>
> —Joshua 1:9

DAY 9

Match Your Stride

When a herd of horses is traveling somewhere in a hurry, they do something called "match their stride." Each horse matches its stride with the horse beside or in front of it, making it so no horse is going too fast or too slow. Now, if we turn on our "horse-seeing" eyes, we can see that our friendships can be just like a herd of wild horses. Everyone is different, but we are all going somewhere. On our way, we are given a choice, and we can either match our stride with someone or set our own pace.

We all have friends, right? Some of us may have more than others. But besides God and our families, friends are the most important things to us on this earth. Friends can encourage us, make us laugh, be our shoulder to cry on, and sometimes give us the kick in the pants if we need it. They are who we match our stride with, just like our horses do when they are traveling together. The problem is, sometimes, they match their stride with a lazy or slow horse, and it slows the whole herd down because of it.

I don't know about you, but I know I've matched my stride with the wrong person before, and instead of encouragement and laughs, I got torn down and started feeling bad. We need friends to speed us up and to keep us on the right track in our walk with God; otherwise, like a herd of horses matching the wrong stride, we slow down. So, be wise when choosing your friends. They can make all the difference.

Q: Have you ever made the wrong choice of who you match your stride with? How did it make you feel? Compare the changes when you have good influences and when you have bad.

Challenge: If you are truly focused on what matters in life, like prayer and hard work, others will match their stride to yours. Ask God to help you be a good influence so that you can help others speed up their stride in their walk with the Lord (Heb. 10:24).

As iron sharpens iron, so one person sharpens another.

—Proverbs 27:17

DAY 10

Following the Trainer

Have you ever heard of *join up*? *Join up* is an exercise that many trainers use to connect with a horse for the first time. Some horses are harder to join up with than others, but if it's done correctly, the horse should follow the trainer everywhere they go.

You see, when you first meet a horse, they believe they are in charge, and that does not change unless you give them a reason to. A horse will not give you the authority unless it trusts you. Join up is an exercise that helps you show your horse that it can trust you. You can't make a horse trust you; it has to do that on its own. So, it's the trainer's job to make that choice easier for the horse. It's a difficult process sometimes, but once you have a horse's trust, everything gets easier.

Have you figured out why I'm explaining all of this to you? This is the part where I tell you that it somehow has to do with our lives, and it does. Just like our horses, before we have a relationship with our trainer, God, we are in charge of our own lives. But when we accept Him, He takes charge of our lives. That doesn't mean He makes us do it. He gives us a choice; we always have a choice. He doesn't twist our arm and force us to repent, and now we do His will like it's a chore. No! He lays it all out there and gives us a choice. But He also makes it very clear where we will end up if we don't choose Him. In the Bible, it says that "the wages of sin is death." A wage is something you get for doing something. The payment I receive for working my jobs is my wages. So, in other words, the payment for sinning is death. In Romans 3:23, it tells us that "all have sinned and fallen short."

We all deserve death for the sins that we have committed. Thank goodness the story doesn't end there; the Bible goes on to tell us that "the gift of God is eternal life." None of us can work our way out of sin. We can never be good enough on our own, no matter how hard we try. The question is, will we let our Master save us?

Q: What do you think keeps you from making that decision of faith?

Challenge: Even if we accept Christ into our lives, we still forget that in order for our lives to be the best that they can be, we have to give Him control of *every* part of our lives. Think of an area of your life where you're not following the trainer. Pray and give that area of your life to Him, so that your whole life can be focused and following the trainer.

> But God demonstrates His own love for us in this:
> While we were still sinners, Christ dies for us.

—Romans 5:8

DAY 11

Blind Trust

There are hundreds of different styles of riding and all sorts of events: dressage, jumping, barrel racing, cutting, pleasure, endurance racing, and the list could go on and on. I enjoy doing many different events with my horse, but I think one of my favorites is showjumping. Showjumping can be a very challenging event, and not all horses are meant to be jumpers. It takes an extremely smart and agile horse to jump, but what matters most when you're jumping is trust and willingness. You see, horse's eyes are set on the sides of their head, not facing forward like ours. It makes it so they can't see what is directly in front of them. When a horse approaches a jump, he can see it coming. But, as soon as it gets right in front of him, it goes into his blind spot and disappears. So, when a horse jumps, it knows the jump is there, it just doesn't know where. So, the rider has to show him. That's why so many horses stop or refuse to go over a jump because they can't see it and are afraid.

Do you see where I'm going with this one? Sometimes, we are afraid because we can't see what's ahead of us. We don't know what's going to happen in our lives, only God knows that. It's hard to put our trust in someone we can't see, especially when we don't know what's going to happen in our lives. In the Bible, there is story after story about men and women who had to put their trust in God and let Him control their lives. They were afraid, just like we and our horses sometimes, but they trusted in what they couldn't see, and they jumped.

We are afraid of things we can't see, we aren't certain of why things happen, and we fear what is going to happen in the future. God tells us in His word that He will never leave us or forsake us. God even goes on to say that His plans are not to harm us, but to give us hope, and a future (Jer. 29:11). We don't need to worry about what's in front of us because God's got it. We just need to have faith and trust enough to jump, even when we can't see.

Q: Do you ever worry about the future, or about things that are beyond your control?

Challenge: I don't know about you, but I know I worry about the future a lot. Every time you catch yourself worrying or over planning for the future, try praying about those worries instead. Remember the horse's trust, and then jump! God will guide you.

So we fix our eyes not on what is seen,
but on what is unseen, since what is seen is temporary,
but what is unseen is eternal.

—2 Corinthians 4:18

DAY 12

Facing the Fear

Let's review a few of the points that we have learned in the past few days. We learned about following our Master no matter how bad things get and the blind trust that we must have in order to do that. We also learned about our natural response to fear and how hard it is to face. A few days ago, I explained that the only way to get rid of fear is to face it. It's the same way we teach our horses; however, it's way easier to say it than to do it, isn't it? We can talk about facing our fears all we want, but if we don't ever face them, they will never go away. So how do we get ourselves to do what scares us the most and face our fear?

I give riding lessons to a few girls and one of the first things they learn from me is this—the more you think about something, the scarier it gets. If I know something is possibly going to scare me while I'm riding, I try to do it as fast as I can so that my body can't react to how scared I actually am. See, when you get scared, your body gets all tense and even freezes sometimes. When you freeze or tense up, your horse feels it, and they freeze. So when my girls are scared or nervous, I encourage them to say a prayer and then just do it! No stalling, very little thinking, and lots of faith and courage; your body and the horse do the rest. A very famous man named John Wayne once said that "courage is being scared to death, but choosing to saddle up anyway."

Shouldn't we live our whole lives like that? The world is full of terrifying things, and the devil will never stop planting fear in our minds to keep us from doing what God wants us to do. The sooner we learn to trust God with our fears, the sooner we can get over them.

Q: What is keeping you from facing your fear?

Challenge: Think about what is holding you back from facing your fear. Pray and ask the Lord to take it away and then trust Him, and just do it! Face your fear!

When I am afraid, I put my trust in you.

—Psalm 56:3

DAY 13

Powerful Love

Horses are really strong and amazing animals, but have you ever thought about how strong they really are? These "pets" of ours can weigh thousands of pounds and could easily crush us if they wanted to. Some of them can easily be a foot taller than us, and those hooves of theirs could do some serious damage. Not to mention, horses are unpredictable creatures, which means you never know what they are thinking. Sure, we guess what they are thinking, and with time, we get pretty good at guessing, but we never know what they are truly thinking and that makes them more dangerous.

Horses are powerful, but yet, they still have a love in their hearts that's even more powerful. Most of the time, that love makes us forget about how dangerous they are. Now, if we put on our "horse-seeing" eyes, I think we'll see that our Father God is a lot like our horses in this area. He is very strong! God is strong enough to part an entire ocean in half (Exod. 14), strong enough to shoot fire from heaven and destroy a whole city (Gen. 19), and strong enough to roll the stone away from His own grave (Mark 16).

Our God is the most powerful being in the universe, and yet He is still the most loving as well. He is loving enough to make bread fall from the sky to feed His people (Exod. 16), and to give up His own son to die a painful death so that we could live with Him forever (John 3). The beautiful and yet powerful love your horses have is the same kind of powerful love our God has for us except God can stop our hearts from beating anytime He wants; however, He doesn't because He loves us. He's like a dad rooting for His child. God is the only one who is all-powerful, but is also the only one who is all-loving. So, the next time you doubt your worth or your purpose, remember your all-powerful, all-loving God is rooting for you.

Q: Are you like me and forget about how powerful and loving God is?

Challenge: Think of a person that you think loves you a lot, and then ask yourself this question, "Do they love me more than God does?" the answer will always be "no" because God has done more for you than anyone else on this earth ever could. Always remember that!

God is exalted in His power. Who is a teacher like Him?

—Job 36:22

DAY 14

Running Wild

Now we know horses can be very loving and gentle, but we also know that horses can be incredibly high strung and wild. Remember, in the very beginning of creation, horses just ran wild, living in herds with no one to keep them safe except themselves. When humans did round them up to train them, the horses fought because they didn't want to lose their freedom, and they didn't want to be owned by anyone, but once they were broke and learned how to trust, they came to enjoy the safety of the human's fences and barns.

Can't we humans be a lot like that at times? I know I can be! I enjoy the idea of running free and controlling my own life, but that's not what God has planned for me nor you. When we accept Him, He becomes our Master and builds "fences" to keep us safe from temptations of this world. He gave us jobs to do and rules to follow, which are all in His word; the Ten Commandments and the golden rule are a couple examples (Exod. 34).

God created these rules, these "fences," to keep us safe so that we can glorify Him with our lives. He didn't make them to trap us or to break us. He did it because He loves us and wants what is best for us. I don't know about you, but that makes me feel a little different about breaking out and running wild. God will always be our protector, and His fences will always stand. We just have to decide to either stay inside them or run wild.

Q: What temptations are leading you outside of God's fences?

Challenge: Sometimes, God uses other people or things to remind you where His fence is. Pray and ask God to make you more aware of the "fences" He's created for you, and be respectful of them.

For this is the love of God, that we keep His commandments.
And His commandments are not burdensome.

—1 John 5:3

DAY 15

The Bit

Do you know where the most sensitive part of the horse is? I'll give you a hint—it's also one of the main things we use to control them. If you guessed the mouth, then you would be right. The horse's mouth is the most sensitive part of a horse, but it's also where we control a lot of their movement. With a simple little iron rod in our horse's mouths, we can tell them where to go and when to stop. The most important thing about the mouth is the softer the horse's mouth is to the bit, the easier it is to control them. The very first thing I teach a new horse is to have a soft mouth, so they can respond to my commands better. They should be able to turn left and right with the flick of a finger.

Isn't that how our relationship with God should be? We should be so sensitive and willing to follow His direction. I know a lot of times I pray and ask God for direction, and then I don't even listen for the answer, much less follow it. Could you imagine if our horses just decided not to respond to us anymore? We would get angry and want to give up.

Lucky for us, God never gives up on us, and He gives us directions over and over again (Jer. 33:3). Just like teaching a horse to have a soft mouth, it takes a lot of hard work and concentration to be able to listen to God and His Holy Spirit, but with a lot of prayers and a "soft mouth," His will can be heard, and we can live it.

Q: Do you ever have a "hard mouth" toward God? Why do you think that is?

Challenge: Let's stop ignoring God's will and soften our mouths to what He has to say. When you pray or read your Bible, really try to focus on what God could be showing you.

> He replied, "Blessed rather are those who
> hear the word of God and obey it."

—Luke 11:28

DAY 16

The Fake Tail

D id you know that some people put fake tails on their horses when they compete? Yes, you heard right, I said fake tail! Just like some people use hair extensions, some people put a fake tail extension inside their horse's real tail to make it look thicker and longer. There's nothing wrong with that. In fact, a lot of judges like it. Between you and me, I enjoy seeing a horse in its natural beauty: clean and nothing added.

That's how I think we humans should be, especially us girls. There are so many lies that are thrown at us girls about the way we should look, how we're supposed to act, and even how we should live. It makes it hard for us to be content with how God made us, but that's all God wants us to do. He tells us to live in the world, but not be *of* the world (1 John 2:15–17). He's basically saying, "I created you this way, you are perfectly made, and nothing you do will make you less than my little girl."

He also tells us that our bodies are the temple of God and that we need to take care of ourselves. It is similar to how we take care of our horses. We need to eat healthily, we need to keep clean, and we need to stay active in life and in His word. If we do those things, there is nothing that could make us more beautiful in His eyes. So, next time you feel like the world is telling you to do something in order to be beautiful or popular, remember that you are already beautifully and wonderfully made and that God loves you just the way you are.

Q: What lies do you hear from the world? How does it make you feel?

Challenge: For the next week, no matter how you feel about yourself, I want you look in the mirror and say out loud, "I am beautifully and wonderfully made." You are beautiful sweet girl, don't let the world tell you any different!

> See what great love the Father has lavished on us,
> that we should be called children of God!
> And that is what we are! The reason the world does
> not know us is that it did not know Him.

—1 John 3:1

DAY 17

Learning the Pattern

N ow no matter what level you ride at, if you compete in just about anything-barrel racing, show jumping, reining, showmanship, there's a really good chance you'll have to memorize some sort of test or pattern chosen by the judge. Then, everything you do in that class is based on that pattern, and if you forget it or mess it up (which I have done before), you most likely won't do very well. All of your chances of success ride completely on you memorizing this pattern and remembering it through the whole class. If you turn your "horse-seeing" eyes on, can you guess what "pattern" in our lives we should be memorizing? If you said the Bible, you would be right. Just like everything rides on how well we know the pattern, everything should be riding on how well we know God's word. The more we know about the Bible, the more we know about God, and the more we know about God, the closer we are to Him (2 Tim. 3:16).

The same way the judge creates the pattern and gives it to us to follow, God used forty different people to write the Bible for us to follow and learn from. It's easy to forget how powerful the Bible is. It is described to be more powerful than the sharpest sword (Heb. 4:12). It is what Jesus himself quoted to fight off the devil (Matt. 4:1–11), and without the Bible, there would be no way to spread the good news of salvation. Without the Bible, we wouldn't even know what the good news is. Let's not disappoint the "judge." Let's start reading and memorizing His "pattern."

Q: How often are you in God's word? Do you ever get distracted? If so, by what?

Challenge: Knowing His word in our heads is just as important as believing it in our hearts. Really try and memorize some scripture and keep it fresh in your mind.

> I have hidden your word in my heart that
> I might not sin against you.

—Psalm 119:11

DAY 18

Deep Pockets

If you haven't figured it out yet, I'm a speed demon when I ride sometimes, and I really enjoy going fast. Barrel racing at a rodeo is one of my favorite weekend activities. I like barrel racing because it's so simple; run around three barrels as fast as you can without tipping them over. Simple, right? Well, for the most part, yes it is simple, but there are a few things that are very important if you want to be a good barrel racer. The most important thing that you need to know in order to be fast is you need deep pockets when you turn your barrels.

The way to make a pocket is to start your turn wide and away from the barrel then, once you pass it, you sit and turn into a little pocket. The tighter your pocket is, the closer you are to the barrel, and the closer you are to the barrel, the faster your time will be. Just like our deep pockets with the barrel, the closer we are to God, the more we understand Him, and the more we understand Him, the better we can serve Him, but when our pockets get wide, and we are far away from God, it makes it hard for us to understand what He wants us to learn, and we slow down.

The Bible tells us to draw near to God, and if we do, we will be blessed (Ps. 65:4). I don't know about you, but I know I want my relationship with God to have "deep pockets." I want to be swift and willing to give Him glory every day.

Q: What about you, do you think your pockets are deep or shallow? What slows you down the most?

Challenge: Pray and ask God to remove whatever it is that slows you down. Ask Him to make you swift and to help give you deep pockets.

Let us approach God's throne of grace with confidence,
so that we may receive mercy and find grace
to help us in our time of need.

—Hebrews 4:16

DAY 19

Brush Down

Before we go riding out on the trail, practice in the arena, or even tack our horses up, there's something we need to do first: a brush down. Whether your horse has been in a stall or in the pasture, he or she has gotten dirty. Brush down is very important, and if we rush or skip it, our horses have a very good chance of getting saddle sores from the dirt rubbing between their back and the saddle pad. Brush down is also a very important time to relax your body and to make sure you have the right mindset before you get in the saddle. How you handle your brush down will determine a lot of what happens on your ride.

The same is true for us. We need our daily quiet times to keep us fresh and focused to follow our Master every day. In John 15:7, God tells us to abide in Him, and He will abide in us. He wants us to get to know Him, to learn about Him, and the only way to do that is to read what He's given to us—the Bible. The Bible is a huge get-to-know-me letter for us from God. The more we read, the more God shows us who He is, and what He wants us to do, which makes glorifying Him so much easier.

See the connection? The same way we start our ride off with a brush down and mindset check, we also need to start our own day the right way by putting God first in our minds. If we do both of those things, everything will go a lot smoother in our ride, and in our lives (Ps. 119:10–11).

Q: How do you normally start each day? Do you think this puts God in the front of your mind?

Challenge: I know how busy our lives can get, but that shouldn't stop us from having our personal time with God. I challenge you to try to start doing your quiet times in the morning, even if you have to get up a few minutes early to give yourself time.

All scripture is God-breathed and is useful for teaching,
rebuking, correcting, and training in righteousness,
so that the servant of God may be thoroughly
equipped for every good work.

—2 Timothy 3:16–17

DAY 20

Barn Sour

H ave you ever seen a barn sour horse? Have you ever ridden one? All they ever do is fight you because all they want to do is go back to the barn. Ever wonder why that is? Well, for the answer to that question, we'll have to go back to their flight nature and how they fear everything. A horse can get barn sour because of several different things, but I believe there is only one reason why, fear! There is fear of the unknown, fear of leaving the known, and fear of not coming back. Horses feel fear before they feel any other emotion, which is why some of them like to cling only to what they know best, the barn.

Now, I'm not saying that we humans get barn sour and never want to leave our barns. (Although it may be true for some of us.) But what about other things like our homes, and our friend groups? I believe there is one big thing that most of us humans are scared to leave, and that's our comfort zone. We all have one, some of them are just bigger than others; either way, we all need a special kind of courage to be able to step out of our comfort zones. If we are followers of Jesus Christ, we need to be willing to step out of that comfort zone on a daily basis, and that's a scary thing (James 1:22). God promises that He will never give us more than we can handle (1 Cor. 10:13), but He also tells us to put our whole faith in Him. That means trusting Him with everything, even if we don't feel comfortable with it.

Are we ready and willing to step out of our comfort zones for the Lord? Or are we like some of our horses, fearful, and refuse to leave our "barns?"

Q: Is there something you refuse to do for fear of leaving your comfort zone?

Challenge: I challenge you to step out of your comfort zone sometime this week. No one has to know about it, and it doesn't have to be huge, just big enough to remind you that you need God's help.

I will lead the blind by ways they have not known,
along unfamiliar paths I will guide them; I will turn the darkness
into light before them and make the rough places smooth.
These are the things I will do; I will not forsake them.

—Isaiah 42:16

DAY 21

Constantly Feasting

Chomp, chomp, chomp! Have you ever sat and watched a horse eat it's hay or graze in the pasture? All they do is chew and swallow, chew and swallow, they never even come up to take a breath. They can go on for hours, even days it feels like! They're bottomless pits that will never be full. No, I'm not saying that we humans are like that. Although I am known to get quite grumpy when I'm hungry, that's not the point. When humans eat, we get full, and we eventually have to stop. Even those big hungry boys eventually get full, but the Bible tells us that we should not live by bread alone (Matt. 4:4).

The most important thing that we need to "eat" each day is a large helping of God's word. No, He's not saying that we need to go hungry and just read the Bible—that's called fasting—and that's definitely not what I'm talking about here. I think what He's trying to tell us is that we should be dependent on the Bible just as much as we are on food every day. Our food feeds our bodies, but the Bible and the Holy Spirit inside us feed our souls, and without that, we quickly forget the real reason we are here.

We should be starving for more knowledge of the Bible every day. Just like our horses, we should be constantly feasting, never getting full, and always chomping on more God-given knowledge.

Q: How often do you read your Bible?

Challenge: Life gets busy, or we forget, but those are not good excuses to skip reading time. Even if you have to ask a friend or parent to remind you to stay in God's word, never stop feasting!

For the Word of God is alive and active.
Sharper than any double-edged sword, it penetrates even to
dividing soul and spirit, joints and marrow;
it judges the thoughts and attitudes of the heart.

—Hebrews 4:12

DAY 22

Sway Back

Have you ever seen a swayback horse? Swayback normally happens when an older horse's back begins to swoop down, showing its old age and how much work it has done with a rider on its back. Sometimes, swaybacks are not very pretty to look at and could eventually cause back problems for the horse. Why am I bringing this up? Because I believe today's lesson is not spoken about enough, let alone learned by many people. Today, we're talking about aging or the elderly. If you're anything like the way I was when I was your age, you sometimes wonder why God would let people get old, especially if they're grumpy. Of course, they're not all bad, but I know I at least. at one point in time, asked, "What does God want with old people? How could He possibly use them for anything?" The same thing could be asked about a swayback horse.

So, what is the answer? What do elderly people have that we young ones don't? Well, in Job 12:12, God tells us this, "Wisdom belongs to the aged, and understanding to the old." So, the first thing, and I think the biggest thing, elderly people have is wisdom. They have lived longer than us and know way more about life than we do. As I have gotten older myself, I have learned to really listen to what elderly people have to teach me, which brings us to another way God uses them. He uses them to teach us so that we can learn from their mistakes, and be encouraged by their triumphs (2 Cor. 4:16).

Just like our swayback horses, the elderly have way more to give than we know. And God continues to use them until the day He calls them home.

Q: How often do you talk with elderly people? Do you ever want to avoid them?

Challenge: Some of the best horses I have ever ridden were swayback, and some of my best conversations were spoken with elderly people. The next time you are around the elderly, ask them some questions. They were once your age too, ya know? Try to learn at least one thing from them.

> Remember the days of old; consider the generations
> long past. Ask your father and he will tell you,
> your elders, and they will explain to you.

—Deuteronomy 32:7

DAY 23

Head Up

Horses are sensitive animals. Even the slightest movements or sounds can set them off, especially if they are your own movements or sounds. Some horses are more sensitive than others, but once a horse is in tune with a rider, they learn to feel everything—the twitch of your hand, the wiggle of your leg, and even the flutter of the nervous butterflies in your stomach. Horses feel everything, and it affects how they act, and most importantly, where they go.

If you ride a horse that can feel even the twitch of your finger, and even know how you feel, you can be sure that they know where you're looking and what you're thinking. One of the many things I say to my rider is this, "Wherever you look, they will go!" Let's say you're on the side of a cliff, and all you had was a path in front of you. On one side, the cliff goes straight down. The other way, the cliff goes straight up. If you look down the cliff, your horse will feel it and lean towards it. The only way to stay on the path is to keep your head straight forward and focused on what's directly in front of you.

The same is true in life, right? There are so many temptations trying to pull us from the path God has for us. The only way we can resist those temptations is by keeping our heads up and focused on what's in front of us: God's plan (Ps. 125:1.) Easier said than done, I know, but try to picture temptations as the cliff. If you so much as look, you'll fall. So, trust your God and keep your eyes fixed on the horizon.

Q: Do you ever feel tempted or pulled down a path that you shouldn't go down? If so, how?

Challenge: Pray and ask God to put a compass inside you and to keep you looking in the direction He wants you to go.

Let your eyes look straight ahead; fix your gaze directly before you.
Give careful thought to the paths for your feet and be
steadfast in all your ways. Do not turn to the right
or to the left; keep your foot from evil.

—Proverbs 4:25–27

DAY 24

The Bucks of Life

Have you ever gotten bucked off, fallen off your horse, or fallen off anything? Not very fun is it? Falling off can be scary and makes us a little more nervous the next time we get on our horse, but even though it's kinda scary, when we fall off, we have to get right back on to show our horse that we will not give up even if we are scared. You know what I'm gonna say next, right? If we turn on our "horse-seeing" eyes, we'll see the same is true in life. Tough things happen, and life bucks us off. We get up and then we may get bucked off again, and we may get discouraged. We feel like we will never beat the bucks of life. God tells us that those bucks happen for a reason, and that if we have faith and trust in Him, He will pick us up and help us through it (Pss. 46:1–3).

The more we fall off our horses, the stronger we get and the easier it is for us to get back up and try again. In life, God gives us the strength to rise up and face the challenges in front of us, even after we fall. That's a hard thing to remember, especially when you're on the hard ground after a big fall. But even there, when you want to give up, God can help you get back on and try again. In the end, it makes success much more rewarding.

Q: Has life ever knocked you down? Did it make it harder for you to get back up?

Challenge: The next time life bucks you off, while you're down, thank the Lord for always being there to help you back up. After that, brush yourself off and try again.

> For though the righteous fall seven times, they rise again,
> but the wicked stumble when calamity strikes.

—Proverbs 24:16

DAY 25

Check Yourself

Have you ever seen a horseplay tug-of-war? No, I'm not kidding. My horse plays tug-of-war all the time, although it's probably not like what you're picturing in your head. When a horse plays tug-of-war, it simply means that they pull on the bit and force the rider to pull back to keep them from going too fast. This causes a lot of problems, especially for a young horse, because if the reins are loose, they end up getting ahead of themselves and doing something they didn't mean to do.

What I like to do to fix this problem is called "check and release." When they start getting ahead of themselves, I can "check" them by pulling them down to the speed I want. As soon as they reach that speed, I let them try again. With the young or hyper horses, I have to check them hundreds of times before they understand.

Now, I don't know about you, but that sure sounds a lot like me when I was younger. I was always getting into trouble because I didn't think before I acted. Even now, I catch myself getting ahead of everything and forgetting about God's plan. I play tug-of-war between my ideas for my life and God's will for my life. It sounds silly when you put it into words. God gave us the Holy Spirit to "check" us when we get ahead of ourselves, and sometimes. that can be hard to obey. I know I'm still learning how *not* to play tug-of-war with God when He "checks" me. But once we learn to trust the "check," the better off we'll be (James 5:7–8).

Q: Do you every get ahead of yourself and play tug-of-war with God or someone else?

Challenge: As you get older, waiting on God's plan gets harder and harder, so I challenge you now to start practicing by praying and listening for His "check."

> The Lord is good to those whose hope is in
> Him, to the one who seeks Him.

—Lamentations 3:25

DAY 26

Ask

Now I have a question for you, how good are you at asking for help? I'm gonna tell you something that I'm not proud of. I am awful at asking for help, even when I know I need it. My prideful spirit gets the best of me more than I'd like, and it's made me learn lessons the hard way, especially when it came to horses. I was so prideful, my mom and sister didn't even want to try to help me because I was sure I knew everything already. When I was wrong, I would come up with an excuse or blame someone else. Looking back on it now, I really regret being so prideful and not listening to anyone because it made me miss out on a lot of beautiful things.

What I'm slowly getting around to saying is, that when you do something like ride horses, there are always new things to learn. If you're like how I was, and too prideful to accept that, you miss out on a lot and can't ride to your fullest potential. And guess what? That's also true in real life. We're always going to have more to learn and more to overcome, and the easiest way of doing that is by admitting that we don't know it all. We learn to accept help and constantly ask the Lord for His guidance and help (Prov. 21:1).

I still struggle to ask for help sometimes, and I know that I will always go through life trying to get better at it. This is why we need the Lord so bad and that's why we need to be humble enough to ask Him for Help. He knows we need it. He just waits for us to realize it.

Q: Have you ever been too prideful or embarrassed to ask someone for help?

Challenge: Asking for help is sometimes harder than figuring something out yourself because it forces you to admit you need help. Next time you try to avoid help, remember some of the greatest people that ever lived asked for help, but they only became great after God helped them.

> Whoever heeds discipline shows the way of life, but
> whoever ignores correction leads others astray.

—Proverbs 10:17

DAY 27

The Love of the Master

My horse is my best friend. His name is Bow, and he's always there for me to talk to and work with. He's still pretty young and get excited about anything, so he can be a bit of a handful sometimes, but no matter how much work he is, he's still my favorite horse, and I will always love him. I bought him because I saw something special, and I'll keep working with him and loving him until that special something comes out and shines.

The love of a master is something that doesn't go away very easily. If you have a horse, or any kind of pet to master over, you understand what I'm talking about, and you may see where this lesson is going. Just like our horses, it doesn't matter what we do to displease God. He will always love us no matter what. If we confess our many sins, He will always forgive us, and He always has our best interests in mind. Our strong love for our horses is still imperfect, and we get angry or lose our patience, but our Master's love for us is perfect and never goes away. God showed the true meaning of love when He sent His son to die on the cross to save us when we didn't love Him in return (John 4:19).

The love of our Savior makes our love for our horses look like silly puppy love. Let's strive to love the way Jesus loved. Not only to our pets but to everyone around us.

Q: Do you ever struggle to show love to your pet or the people around you?

Challenge: I challenge you to memorize 1 John 4:19, and when you find it hard to love, recite it and remind yourself why we should love in the first place.

We proclaim to you what we have seen and heard, so that you also may have fellowship with us. And our fellowship is with the Father and with His son, Jesus Christ.

—1 John 1:3

DAY 28

Standing Still

Like I said in the last lesson, my horse, Bow, gets excited and a little crazy sometimes. It makes it hard when he needs to stand still for things like getting medicine or getting a wound cleaned. He used to get really anxious and wouldn't let me do what I needed to do even if I was going to help him. It didn't make any sense and all it did was frustrate me.

We humans can be the same way. We can dance around and try to avoid something that scares us even when it will help us or make us a better person in the end. I know I'm guilty of trying to dodge God's will just because it kinda scared me. It always ends up working out for the better though, when I just stand still and let Him do what needs to be done. Sometimes, God sends other people to help us as well, and you know from a few days ago that I struggle with accepting help from other people.

God created us to live our lives in community with other believers. Just like our horses, we are herd creatures and aren't meant to be alone. God made us to help each other and to spur each other on in love and good deeds (Heb. 10:24–25), but that can't happen if we are dancing around because we are too scared to accept anything. We need to be brave and humble and let our lives stand still sometimes. When we do so, God, and other people He sends, can help us and make us better.

Q: Do you ever have trouble standing still? Why do you think that is? Is it fear?

Challenge: Sometimes, God uses us to help other people who may struggle to stand still. First, pray and ask God to give you humility and patience. Second, pray that you would be able to spur the people around you toward love and good deeds. Finally, make a point to be an encouragement to someone today.

> Finally, all of you, be like-minded, be sympathetic,
> love one another, be compassionate and humble.

> —1 Peter 3:8

DAY 29

Flying as One

I've worked with quite a few horses, some more than others. The longer I've worked with a horse, the more we are in sync. When you work with a horse for a long time, you learn each other's quirks and movements. It makes for a beautiful ride when the horse knows what the rider wants and when the rider trusts the horse. When this happens, you seem to become one and then you start to feel like you're flying.

We've learned a lot about God and His will these past few weeks thanks to our horses. Now it's up to us to choose to take what we've learned and use that to figure out what to do next. Sometimes, it's hard to know what's supposed to come next, but as we've learned in the previous pages, God will always be by our side as long as we trust Him.

He is our ultimate Master, and He is teaching us how to fly with Him. All He asks of us is to bring glory to His name and learn from our mistakes. He will do the rest (Isa. 58:11). I don't know about you, but I want to be known as the girl who not only flew on horseback, but who also flew with God and followed after His heart.

Q: Is there anything that's keeping you from launching to the skies with God?

Challenge: Pray and ask God to take away any doubts you may have, and then close your eyes and picture yourself flying on top of your horse with God flying next to you.

Whether you turn to the right or to the left,
your ears will hear a voice behind you,
saying, "this is the way; walk in it."

—Isaiah 30:21

DAY 30

Share the Joy

Well, we made it to day thirty! Through the past thirty days, we learned so many lessons about our Savior and how to follow Him. What do we do now? That's a good question. In Mark 16:15, God tells us the answer. He says to "go into all the world and preach the gospel to all creation." It's a pretty straightforward verse, and yet we go about our days without even thinking about it. I know I don't anyway.

I get all excited and will talk about horses for hours to almost anyone who will listen. It's my passion, my joy, and what helps me get out of my shell. Horses have changed me so much for the better, but as much as horses have given me, God has given me so much more!

God is the one who allowed me to have my horses in the first place. God cared about my desires and helped me make it happen, God protects me all day, every day, and hears every little prayer I think or whisper. God, in all His creativity, thought to create the entire earth and everything in it. He thought to create amazing creatures, like horses, and gives us the ability to communicate and learn from them. God gave us everything—our homes, our families, our pets, and most importantly, He gave us the gift of eternal life. He made a way for us—as sinful as we are—to spend eternity with Him in heaven.

Now if that isn't enough to make you want to talk about Him, I don't know what is!

Q: What will it take to get you to share the good news of Jesus? Do you know someone who doesn't know Jesus?

Challenge: Make it a goal to share the gospel with that one person this next month. It doesn't have to be huge, just share His joy and what He has done for you. If you don't know anyone, pray for an opportunity to spread the joy of the Lord.

Therefore go and make disciples of all nations, baptizing them
in the name of the Father and of the Son and of the Holy Spirit,
and teaching them to obey everything I have commanded you.
And surely I am with you always, to the very end of the age.

—Mathew 28:19–20

ABOUT THE AUTHOR

J essi is an experienced riding instructor who loves teaching young children proper horsemanship, along with real-life lessons. She was raised in simple country living in the boonies of Michigan where she fell in love with being in the midst of God's creation.

CPSIA information can be obtained
at www.ICGtesting.com
Printed in the USA
LVHW010834100521
686963LV00003B/364